Business Plans Made Easy

SUSAN KILMER

CONTENTS

INTRODUCTION

I wanted to start off by thanking you (the reader) for taking an interest in my guide. The main purpose of writing this brief guide is to help both the aspiring entrepreneur and seasoned business owner alike better understand the business planning process.

The average entrepreneur and small business owner knows at very minimum level that they need to write a business plan for one reason or another, but very few understand why which is the main cause as to why it is seen as one of the most difficult pieces of owning a small business.

My goal for this brief guide is for each of you who choose to purchase this book, to better understand the basics of a business plan, why it is important and how to navigate through this seemingly difficult process.

Enjoy!

CHAPTER 1
WHAT IS A BUSINESS PLAN?

At its very essence, a business plan is a roadmap - a guide outlining your designed strategy of starting and operating the business that you have or would like to start (your destination), who you are going to operate it with, how you will fit into an existing marketplace, what need the products or services within your business will solve, who you will sell to and how much it will cost you to start and/or operate.

Do not get hung up on the notion that writing a business plan is a long arduous process, because it doesn't have to be. Don't get me wrong, while it is important to write a business plan - it isn't necessarily a *must do* for being successful with your business venture but it is highly recommended as it helps keep you and your business operations in check if you follow it closely but are open to revising and evaluating it as you go.

A typical business plan is more than bullet points in an outline, or scribble you may have already jotted down on a napkin while have a latte at your local coffee shop. It is detailed document that assists you with developing your business idea and operations more thoroughly. It is also a document that you should refer to more than just at the start of your business.

Unfortunately, most people think business plans are only for starting a new business or applying for funding from your local financial institution, but business plans are also

SUSAN KILMER

important for a business that is currently in operation. Even worse, an even greater number of people do not understand why they should write one, they just know that they should.

CHAPTER 2
WHY IS IT IMPORTANT?

There are several reasons why it is important to write a business plan:

1) You want to have a greater understanding of the direction you want to go in your business and any possible outcomes. It is a lot easier and less stressful having an idea of what your business will be doing in the future - a week, month or even a year from now. It isn't fun running your business day-to-day standing there waiting and hoping that someone, anyone will want to buy from you and will it be enough to cover your expenses at the end of the month.

2) It will be required by 3rd parties you are seeking assistance from whether it be financial instructions, potential business partners, venture capitalists, investors or potential landlords. Anyone who is smart will ask you for your business plan before they should consider dealing with you and your business to assess the potential risks they may encounter and vice versa.

Before we begin, let's go over some Frequently Asked Questions (FAQ):

1) How long does it have to be?

There is no hard fast rule about how long a business plan should be. The important thing is that your business plan should basically give its reviewer a better understanding about:

- The purpose of your business
- How is your business different?
- Who will be working in the business
- What is the environment of the marketplace you are entering into?
- Who you will be selling to,
- What is your strategy in getting these potential customers to buy?
- What it will cost you to start and operate this business and
- What revenue do you expect to earn.

2) Do I really need to write a business plan?

You actually do not, but it is highly recommended. As explained in the previous chapter, there are some businesses who are successful without having a plan or clear direction but those businesses are far and few between and not having a plan eventually catches up to them when things they cannot control happen.

3) When do I write a business plan?

At any time. The sooner the better. Ideally, you will have written it before you launch your business but if you are currently in business and haven't written one yet, now is a good time to write one!

The key point I want to make is, that writing a business plan is not a one-time thing. You will want to review it every so often to make sure your business is on track and especially when you see trends in your industry changing or you are changing your business by expanding or adding new products/services.

4) Where can I get help writing a business plan?

If you are needing help with writing a business plan because you find yourself not exactly skilled at writing, I recommend you do not put the responsibility on someone outside of yourself. They aren't the business owner: YOU ARE. You are the sole source of information of where YOU want the business to head, not a paid business plan writer.

With enough training, determination and persistence - you can be good at writing a business plan. I recommend taking business plan writing classes from your local business development center.

If you are looking for an expert or a business professional to review your business plan and give you feedback, you can inquire with your local business development center as well who have business experts that can explain to you the gaps within your business planning. Some of these business development centers offer assistance at low or no cost.

They can be reached at www.absdc.org, www.score.org or www.sba.gov . While there are numerous organizations that can assist you with developing your business plan, the aforementioned links are one of the most reputable and the best part is their services are primarily offered at **NO COST** to you.

5) Where can I find examples?

There is a wealth of business planning articles and templates online. Just use your preferred search engine. Word of advice: Do copy another individual's business plan examples. They put a lot of hard work into creating samples. Once again I repeat, they aren't the owner of your business: YOU ARE.

6) What do I put in a business plan?

In the following chapters, we will go into more depth regarding some of the most important sections included in a typical business plan:

- **Executive Summary**
- **Company Description**
- **Products/Services**
- **Market Analysis, Plan and Strategy**
- **Organization and Management Team**
- **Financial Plan and Projections**

CHAPTER 3
COVER PAGE AND TABLE OF CONTENTS

The cover page of your business plan should cover any business identifiers such as: business logo, your name and business name, contact information such as telephone and email address, revision number, date and business website address.

There also needs to be table of contents with correlating page numbers. There is nothing worse to a business plan reviewer, investor, potential partner or lending institution than having to find and flip through pages finding the information in your business plan that *they* care about.

You can obtain great logos at websites such as: www.logomyway.com and www.99designs.com Although I have never used either services nor am I affiliated with either one, I have heard numerous positive reviews about the results business owners get from these two sites.

With your business name you will need at the very minimum do a DBA search to see if the name you want to use for the business you would like to be start is currently used within your current county. Each county's clerk recorder website typically has a DBA name search. It is recommended you do this before you file.

Chapter 4
EXECUTIVE SUMMARY

Although the executive summary is the first section of your business plan, it is written last. It is because the executive summary is just that - a summary of your entire business plan. How can you write a summary of a business plan that you haven't written yet? Thus, once you finish writing your entire business plan, you write your executive summary.

The executive summary is a summary of the main sections of your business plan and any related key points. This is usually the first part of your plan that prospective investors and lenders (besides the financial section) will read and it must be interesting, clear and concise otherwise they will not read the rest of the business plan especially the financial section.

Chapter 5
COMPANY DESCRIPTION

This section of your business plan should provide an overview of the business background and history. The company description section of your business plan is typically the second section, coming after the executive summary. The company description outlines vital details about your company, such as where you are located, how large the company is, what you do and what you hope to accomplish.

This is similar to a sales pitch and can help anyone who reads it quickly understand the goal of your business and its differentiation. This will also be the section where you indicate company goals, objects, mission and vision.

What to Include in Your Company Description

- Describe your business and list the marketplace needs that you are trying to solve.
- Explain how your products and services meet these needs.
- List the specific consumers and/or end users (target market) your business will serve.
- Explain the competitive advantages that you believe will make your business a success such as the value provided to your customers.

Chapter 6
PRODUCTS AND SERVICES

This section helps you to think about your product or service which reflects on your ability to understand your clients' expectations. Start with a detailed description of your product or service including what features it offers and how it distinguishes itself from other products or services that already exist in the market place.

Next start describing three unique selling points offered by your product or service and how will they satisfy client needs and expectations.

Key questions to answer in this section:

- What makes your products or services different?
- Are there any competitive advantages and disadvantages compared with offerings from other competitors?
- Is price an issue and will your operating costs be low enough to allow you to make a profit?

Remember, the primary goal of your business plan is to convince you that the business is viable--and to create a road map for you to follow.

Chapter 7
MARKET ANALYSIS

Market research is critical to business success. A detailed business plan analyzes and evaluates customer demographics, purchasing habits and much more.

Start with understanding your market--and the opportunities within that market. This requires answering more thoroughly questions that will help you better understand that market. Evaluate the market at a relatively high level, answering some tough questions about your market and your industry:

- What is the size of the market and is the overall industry growing, stable, or in decline?
- What segment of the market do you plan to target and what demographics and behaviors make up the market you plan to target?
- Is the demand for your specific products or services increasing or declining and can you differentiate yourself from the competition in a way that is important to your target customers? If so, can you differentiate yourself in a cost effective manner?
- What do customers expect to pay for your products or services?

For the market you hope to serve, determine data such as:

- What is your market? Include demographics and psychographic information
- What segment of the market will you focus on? A

specific niche?
- What percentage of the market do you hope to penetrate?
- What is the size of your intended market and the spending habits and levels?
- What do those customers need and why would they be willing to purchase your products and services?
- How will you price your products and services? Will you be the low cost provider or value added at a higher price?

The key is to define your market and then show how you will serve your market. Providing great products and services is great, but customers must actually know those products and services exist otherwise how they will buy which is why strategic marketing plans are critical to your business success.

Chapter 8
ORGANIZATION AND MANAGEMENT TEAM

The next step in creating your business plan is to develop an Operations Plan that will serve your customers, keep your operating costs in line, and ensure profitability. It should detail strategies for managing, staffing, manufacturing, fulfillment, and inventory.

Your goal is to answer the following key questions:

- What facilities, equipment, and supplies do you need?
- What is your organizational structure? Who is responsible for which aspects of the business?
- Is research and development required, either during start-up or as an ongoing operation? If so, how will you accomplish this task?
- What are your initial staffing needs? When and how will you add staff?
- Who will you establish business relationships with vendors and suppliers? How will those relationships impact your day-to-day operations?

Operations plans should be highly specific to your industry, your market sector, and your customers. Instead of providing an example like I've done with other sections, use the following to determine the key areas your plan should address:

- Location and Facility Management
- Zoning requirements
- The type of building you need

- The space you need
- Power and utility requirements
- Parking
- Construction or renovations
- Daily Operations
- Production and Service Methods including sales and customer service
- Licenses and permits
- And much more!

Chapter 9
FINANCIAL PLAN AND PROJECTIONS

Numbers tell the story. Bottom line results indicate the success or failure of any business. Financial projections and estimates help you objectively evaluate your business' potential for success. If you seek outside funding, providing comprehensive financial reports and analysis is critical.

But most importantly, financial projections tell you whether your business has a chance of being viable--and if not let you know you have more work to do. Most business plans include at least five basic reports or projections:

- **Balance Sheet:** Describes the company cash position including assets, liabilities, shareholders, and earnings retained to fund future operations or to serve as funding for expansion and growth. It indicates the financial health of a business.

- **Income Statement:** Also called a Profit and Loss statement, this report lists projected revenue and expenses. It shows whether a company will be profitable during a given time period.

- **Cash Flow Statement:** A projection of cash receipts and expense payments. It shows how and when cash will flow through the business; without cash, payments (including salaries) cannot be made.

- **Operating Budget:** A detailed breakdown of income and expenses; provides a guide for how the company will operate from a "dollars" point of view.

- **Break-Even Analysis**: A projection of the revenue required to cover all fixed and variable expenses. Shows when, under specific conditions, a business can expect to become profitable.

That is pretty much it. A business plan in a nutshell – made to be understood and easy to create. The main thing to understand is that a business plan doesn't need to be a daunting thing, it is merely a document that indicates what your business will be or is about, who currently runs it, what you are selling, who you are selling to, how much it is costing you to do it and how much are you earning in return.

However clear you can describe that without using fluff, the better your business plan will be. Remember: Keep it simple and accurate.

THE END.

I wanted to thank all of you for taking the time to read this guide. I do hope it gave you a clear explanation of what a business plan is, why it is important, what goes in it and most of all what you are supposed to explain in each relevant section.

I do hope you enjoy the book and if you could take the time and review the book. Reviews help me become aware of what you enjoyed and didn't enjoy within the book and what you would like for me to improve. For those of you who want to review the book, you can do so at its appropriate Kindle Page:

http://www.amazon.com/Business-Plan-Writing-Success-Template-ebook/product-reviews/B015XBEQL4/ref=cm_cr_dp_see_all_summary?ie=UTF8&showViewpoints=1&sortBy=byRankDescending#

Thank you.